Please read the pictures of this 1967 story clockwise — and, watch out — do not attempt to climb any watchtowers unless you are a time-served clock-repairer!

Printed and Published in Great Britain by D. C. Thomson & Co., Ltd., 185 Fleet Street, London, EC4A 2HS.
© D. C. THOMSON & CO., LTD., 2005.
ISBN 1 84535 040 5

(Certain stories do not appear exactly as originally published.)

22.2.64

Throw one bald Head and one jaded Teacher into a well-used school, add a sprinkling of Kids, mix well for two pages . . . a perfect recipe for laughter! School dinners have moved on since this Bash Street Kids story — but not all of them were thrown across the tables!

A DEPUTATION OF BASH ST. MUMS APPROACHES THE HEAD WITH A PROPOSAL.

WE'RE FED UP OF OUR HUNGRY KIDS EATIN' US OUT OF HOUSE AN' HOME. WHY DON'T YOU START SCHOOL DINNERS?

LADIES, PLEASE CALM YOURSELVES.

START SCHOOL DINNERS

BAN THE PIGS

SO THE HEAD DISCUSSES THE PROPOSAL WITH THE SCHOOL GOVERNORS AND THEY DECIDE TO START SCHOOL DINNERS AT BASH ST. SCHOOL.

GET THOSE SPUDS PEELED, TEACHER. WE HAVE TO HAVE DINNER READY BY ONE O'CLOCK.

BOILER HOUSE
KITCHEN
HEAD CHEF
TEA LEAF
TEA URN

AT THE SERVING HATCH—

ONE AT A TIME, PLEASE – GLUG!

COAL
SERVING HATCH
PULL
ZINC BATH
TRIP

THAT AFTERNOON, TEACHER GIVES THE CLASS LESSONS IN TABLE MANNERS.

TAKE THE KNIFE IN THE RIGHT HAND AND THE FORK IN THE LEFT HAND . . . . LEFT HAND, HERBERT, YOU NIT.

THEN EAT DAINTILY, SO...

HAVE SOME VINEGAR WITH YOUR DIN-DIN, OL' CHAP.

DELICATE CHOMP

PRANG!

CRUNCH!

BITE

R-R-RIP!

WHEN TEACHER RETURNS TO HIS SEAT, DANNY, WHO IS UNDER THE GOVERNORS' TABLE, PUTS HIS PLAN INTO ACTION.

29.9.62

I'LL JUST POP THESE MICE UP TEACHER'S AN' HEAD'S SLEEVES.

EOOW! EEK!

YAHOO! ARGH!

THE MASTERS' TABLE MANNERS ARE DISGUSTING!

TINY SLOO

SIP

SCHO
SHAME HUMBLE

I WANT MY PUDDING!

HERE, TAKE MINE—IT'S 'ORRIBLE!

THEN—
DIRECT PIPELINE FROM SOUP POT

SLOP! BURP!

DISGUSTIN' MANNERS.

GOT THAT FLY!

SLABBER! SLURP! GOBBLE!

HELP!

'S TOO HOT!

BREEZE

CLINK SLOO! SLURP! BURP!

BOP!

TUT! TUT! THEIR TABLE MANNERS ARE DISGUSTING. YOU MUST SEE THAT THEY IMPROVE BECAUSE I'VE INVITED THE SCHOOL GOVERNORS TO LUNCHEON TOMORROW.

SCHOOL PUD

THAT NIGHT, DANNY HOLDS A SUMMIT CONFERENCE ON TOP OF THE SLAG-HEAP.

COR! I DIDN'T THINK THEY'D BE WORKIN' OVERTIME. NEVER MIND, WE'LL HAVE SOME FUN AT THE GOVERNORS' LUNCHEON TOMORROW. NOW HERE'S WHAT WE'LL DO, BZZZ....

NEXT DAY AT THE GOVERNORS' LUNCHEON—
AH, I'M GLAD TO SEE THAT THE CHILDREN ARE ON THEIR BEST BEHAVIOUR.

WHAT WELL-BEHAVED PUPILS! ALL I NEED NOW IS A GOOD MEAL.

TEACHER'S PLACE

GOLDEN SILENCE

SMUG

I'LL CARVE THE TURKEY NOW. OOPS! WHERE HAS DANNY GONE TO?

GONE

HISS! JAB

HISS!

DISGUSTING EXHIBITION! WE'LL CUT THE MASTERS' FOOD ALLOWANCE FOR THAT, AND WE SHAN'T LET YOU NEAR THE KIDS' FOOD EITHER.

YOU'LL HEAR MORE ABOUT THIS INCIDENT. GOOD DAY!

SNIGGER

SO THE GOVERNORS EMPLOY FRED CRUMPET, THE CHEF FROM THE RITZ HOTEL, TO COOK FOR THE KIDS.

CERTAINLY.

BREAD AND WATER! UGH!

CAN I HAVE A TENTH HELPING OF PUD, PLEASE?

CHOMP CHOMP

YUM YUM

MASTERS ALLOWANCE

WATER

'60S

Hasn't Dirty Dick heard of automatic washer/driers? Well, no, 'cos it was all manual labour in 1967!

JONAH

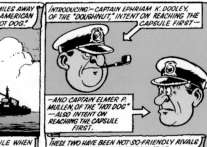

Astronaut John Glenn was in orbit round the Earth in February 1962. Four months later, in The Beano, it looked as if the only safe place for naval nitwit Jonah might be in space, too!

2.6.62

15.12.62

The first series of Brassneck appeared in the Dandy from 5.12.64 right through to 24.2.68. There are "signs" of laughter in the episode below, when Charlie and his metal pal slip into "mirth" gear on their bikes!

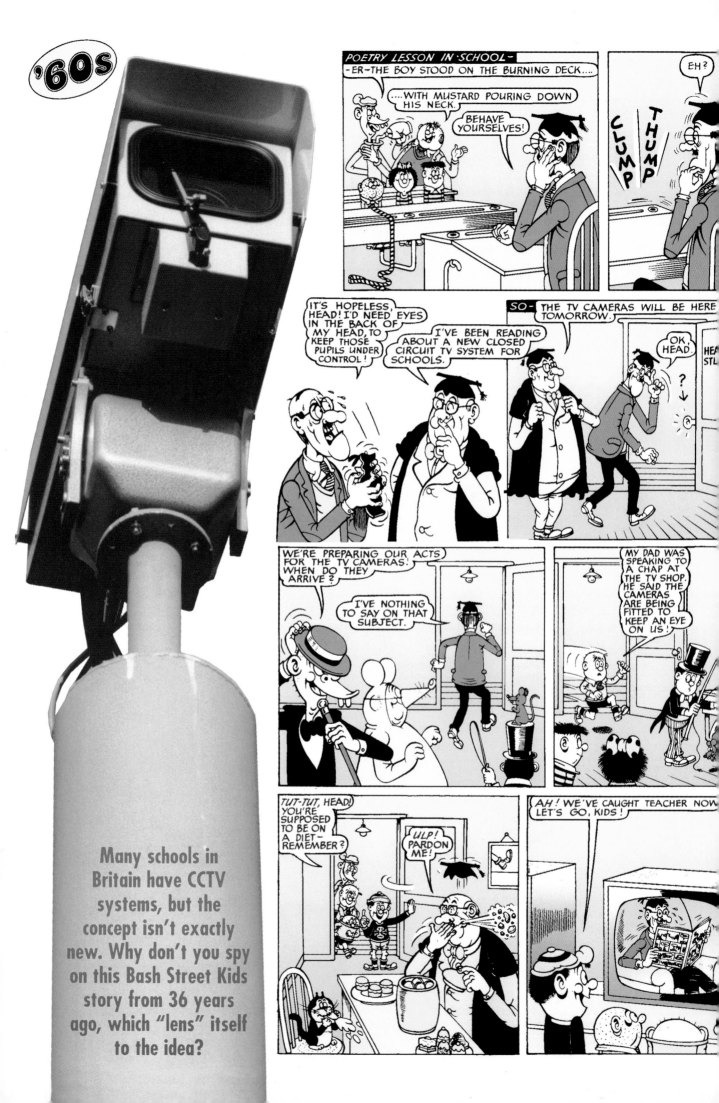

'60s

Many schools in Britain have CCTV systems, but the concept isn't exactly new. Why don't you spy on this Bash Street Kids story from 36 years ago, which "lens" itself to the idea?

8.11.69

Here's a tip for all the Beano and Dandy readers! Actually there are **two** tips, one in each story . . . make that **three**, including the background picture! Anyway, the tip is . . . always separate your rubbish into recyclable and non-recyclable, unless your name is Dirty Dick! As for Dennis, it was a rubbish idea to hide in that cloud of smoke anyway!

JACK DAWSON had a problem—a giant one! He was trying to feed a mouse as big as a horse. The trouble started when an explosion in the chemical works where Jack's father worked spread a liquid called Mixture "G" all over the countryside. The results were frightening, because the heat from the explosion had altered Mixture "G". Now any plant it landed on grew huge, and animals feeding on the plants turned into giants.

Jack had found the giant mouse and brought it home to prevent it running amok all over the countryside. Luckily it was quite tame, and nibbled the loaves Jack was holding out to it.

Suddenly Jack heard terrified scream for he He turned.

Rearing up on its hindlegs it began to tear away the ivy to get at the cheese. Jack at once began to climb up its broad, furry back.

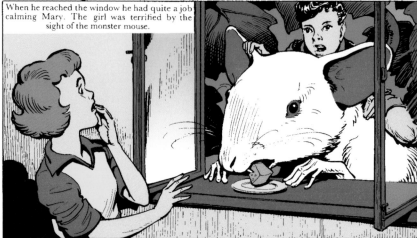

When he reached the window he had quite a job calming Mary. The girl was terrified by the sight of the monster mouse.

Luckily the water was very deep. Soaked, b unhurt, Jack scrambled his knees, just in time to s the mouse scampering through the rushes.

Going like an express train the mouse thundered across a field. Even a duckpond didn't stop its headlong flight. Straight into the pool it plunged with a terrific splash. The mouse's sudden dive unseated Jack and Mary, and they went flying.

Now Jack and Mary were completely encircled by an impenetrable barrier of green spikes. "W-what will we do?" gasped Mary. "We'll never get out, and," she gulped, "and no one knows we're here."

Jack realised only too well that things looked black. But he didn't want to admit he was worried in front of Mary. "I'll soon cut a way out," he said, pulling out his penknife. "Watch." With that he started to hack at the rushes.

It was slow going. After ten minu Jack had only cut through t stems. It would take him ages slash a path through the reeds his knife lasted that long. Sudde Mary gave a terrified gasp. "Lo Look!" she screamed.

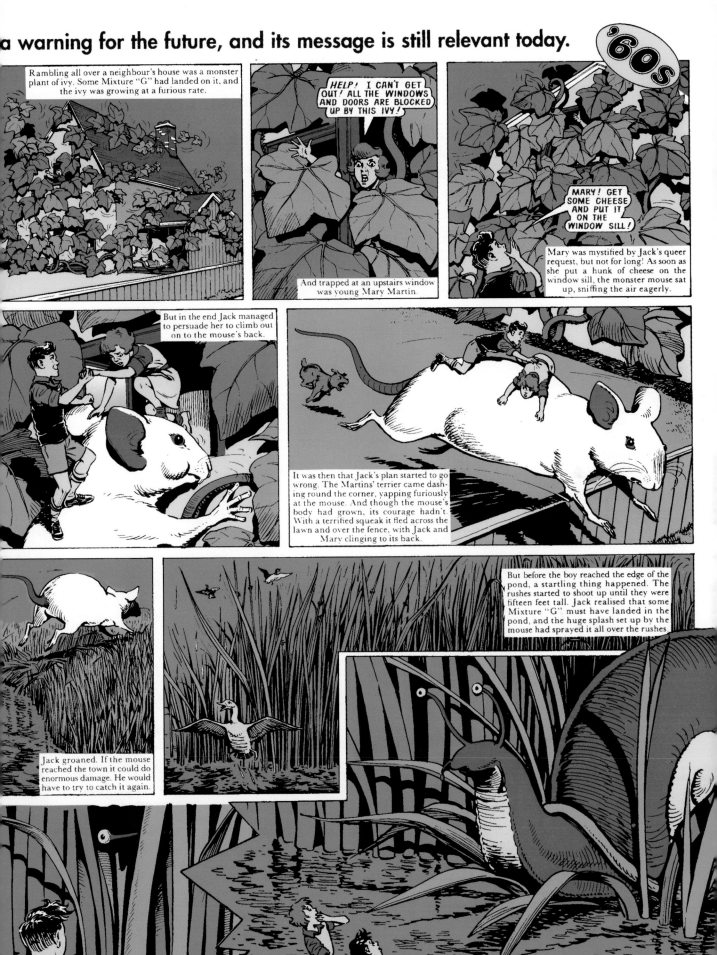

THE Beano AND Dandy TOP TEN FROM THE '60s

3
2
1

There may have been "Three Steps To Heaven" according to Eddie Cochran, back in 1960's music charts, but Minnie the Minx found **her** set of steps led to disaster!

① **THREE STEPS TO HEAVEN** Eddie Cochran

THE Beano AND Dandy TOP TEN FROM THE '60s

One of Petula Clark's many hits in the Sixties was "Sailor".
Did Beano readers at the time think she was singing about their favourite
nautical nincompoop — Jonah — when she sang "Sailor, leave the sea"?

SOMEWHERE, OUT IN THE MED.,
A SUPERB, WHITE YACHT LIES
AT ANCHOR—THE "DASCHUND."

DASCHUND

HEH-HEH! AND SOME
THOUGHTFUL CLOT HAS
LEFT A PORT-HOLE
WIDE-OPEN
FOR
ME!

JONAH

② SAILOR   Petula Clark

3

THE Beano AND Dandy TOP TEN FROM THE '60s

DON'T TREAT ME LIKE A CHILD   Helen Shapiro

By 1962, songs like the above broke records for teenage sensation Helen Shapiro — two Number One hits and three others in the Top Five before she was sixteen years old. Minnie the Minx's voice could only break glass . . .

10.2.62

The velvet-voiced Mr Jim Reeves had a Number One Hit with "Distant Drums" in 1964. In the same year, Lord Snooty's pals wished that Snooty had distant drums too, as they did their best to get rid of them!

25.1.64

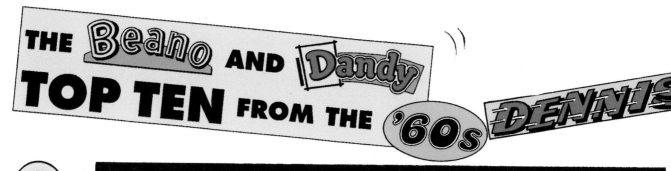

THE Beano AND Dandy TOP TEN FROM THE '60s DENNIS

⑤ DO WAH DIDDY DIDDY Manfred Mann

Manfred Mann's chart topping hit of 1964, "Do Wah Diddy Diddy", sums up this "baby" Dennis story from the same year, where Dad locks Dennis in a pram to keep him out of mischief. Maybe Dennis should re-title the song "Do What? Didn't! Didn't!"

Was Desperate Dan thinking of Marianne Faithfull's 1965 Top Ten hit "This Little Bird" when he was looking for someone to blame for this chaos back in 1969?

6 THIS LITTLE BIRD   Marianne Faithfull

THE Beano AND Dandy
TOP TEN FROM THE '60s

Can you quickly identify the characters from their puppet parts in this figure? Answers below —

ANSWERS:—

Lord Snooty's head.
Body — Pa Bear.
Right arm —
Minnie the Minx.
Left Arm —
Dennis the Menace.
Right leg —
Biffo the Bear.
Left leg —
Billy Whizz.

Sandie Shaw's Eurovision Song Contest winning song in 1967, "PUPPET ON A STRING", was in the charts for over four months. In that same year, the Beano didn't have a Song Contest, but did have puppets. A different cut-out puppet appeared each week for over a year, so that the readers could make their very own Beano Puppet Show!

BiFFO THE BEAR

BIFFO AND BUSTER ARE HAVING SUPER FUN PLAYING WITH THEIR PUPPET SHOW— AND YOU CAN HAVE ONE TOO, READERS! SEE BELOW FOR INSTRUCTIONS.

1 STICK PICTURE ON FIRM CARDBOARD.
2 NEATLY CUT OUT THE PARTS WITH A PAIR OF SCISSORS (CAREFULLY NOW!).
3 BORE HOLES IN THE PLACES MARKED THROUGH THE DOUBLE HOLES
4 LOOP SHORT THREADS THROUGH THE DOUBLE HOLES AND TIE PARTS TOGETHER. (NOT TOO TIGHTLY!).
5 FIT LONG CONTROLLING THREADS TO THE OTHER HOLES IN THE ELBOWS AND TOES—AND WATCH THOSE PUPPETS DANCE AND KICK!

7

PUPPET ON A STRING Sandie Shaw

THE Beano AND Dandy
TOP TEN FROM THE '60s

Korky the Cat had never been "Surfin' USA" like the Beach Boys, but in this 1967 tale, he wanted his chums to get rid of their "bushy blond hairdos" and change their image. (Coincidentally, on a 1967 Beach Boys LP there was a track titled "She's Goin' Bald" — was this where Korky got his idea from?!)

8 SURFIN' USA   The Beach Boys

DANDY JIM BREWSTER

BRODY BREWSTER

C-C

9

PURPLE HAZE   Jimi Hendrix Experience

The Jimi Hendrix Experience's hit single "Purple Haze" didn't quite reach the dizzy heights of the Number One Spot (peaking at Number Three in March '67, with a total of 14 weeks in the Charts) but could this song have been inspired by a story called "The Purple Cloud" which caused chaos and destruction in the cattle lands of the U.S.A. for 36 weeks in The Dandy back in 1961?

THE PURPLE CLOUD

THIS is the story of a strange mystery —the mystery of the Purple Cloud. What it was or where it came from, nobody knew. But wherever it went, it left a trail of destruction through the cattle lands of North America.

Dandy Jim Brewster and his young brother, Brody, managed a ranch, and it was on their land that the strange cloud first made an appearance.

Sure enough, billowing towards them was a strange, purple cloud. Birds fled before it, and the cattle were stampeding in panic.

When the cloud had passed, Jim gasped in horror. Brody and his horse lay on the ground—and both had turned purple!

A FRIGHTENED crowd huddled in the lee of a rock on a cattle ranch in North America. All eyes were riveted on the strange, purple cloud that was drifting towards them. This weird cloud had appeared earlier that day — with terrifying results! For every metal object it passed over was mysteriously melted away.

Dandy Jim Brewster, who ran the ranch, laid a reassuring hand on his young brother's shoulder. "Don't worry, Brody," he said. "The cloud won't harm you! You've no metal about you." That was another oddity about the cloud. Anyone carrying or wearing a metal object was knocked out and turned purple.

With the boy in his arms, Jim rode for home.

And he galloped through fences which every strand of wire had mysteriously disappeared!

Jim led the way to the spot where they had parked their old jalopy. But what a shock they got! All the metal parts had vanished completely! Just the tyres, seats, steering wheel and windscreen remained.

Using his secret weapon, the Purple Cloud, Purple Mask was robbing the banks of North America. The Cloud melted all metals, except silver, and anyone in contact with metal was knocked out and turned purple.

A PLANE droned across the skies above a desert in North America. From it, Dandy Jim Brewster and his brother, Brody, scanned the rolling dunes below. They were searching for a hidden city—headquarters of Purple Mask, the world's master criminal.

At that very moment, Purple Mask was heading for a New York bank. A policeman saw him climb from one of his strange flying saucers.

WHOOSH! Purple Mask fired a blast of Purple Cloud. The policeman fell, unconscious and purple. He had been holding his revolver and the Cloud had struck him down.

THE Beano AND Dandy TOP TEN FROM THE '60s

The Rolf Harris hit "Two Little Boys" was the final chart-topper of the '60s. In the song, "each had a wooden horse", but in this Big Head and Thick Head story from 1967, each had a wooden SAW-horse!

I DON'T KNOW WHAT'S WRONG WITH HIM, BIG HEAD.

HE'S BEEN HAVING A BAD DREAM, THAT'S ALL!

THERE'S MY TICKET—

GRR! I'VE GOT YOU NOW!

OH, NO! NOT YOU!

10 TWO LITTLE BOYS   Rolf Harris

Note for really keen comic fans — the caricatures of the Beatles used on these pages are taken from a Dandy page: My Home Town (Liverpool) issue dated 1.2.64.

The 'Fab Four', as The Beatles were called, influenced many things during the '60's — including The Dandy! On these pages are a 'Fab Three' tales which prove that even long-standing favourites like Dennis the Menace and Korky the Cat experienced the Beatles phenomenon.

5.9.64

Today, hovercraft can be seen mainly in common use as high-speed ferry vehicles, but in the '60s they were seen as something out of science-fiction.

SEND FOR the HOVERTANK

The Beano's "Hovertank" was set to save the world for roughly seven months, back in 1969.

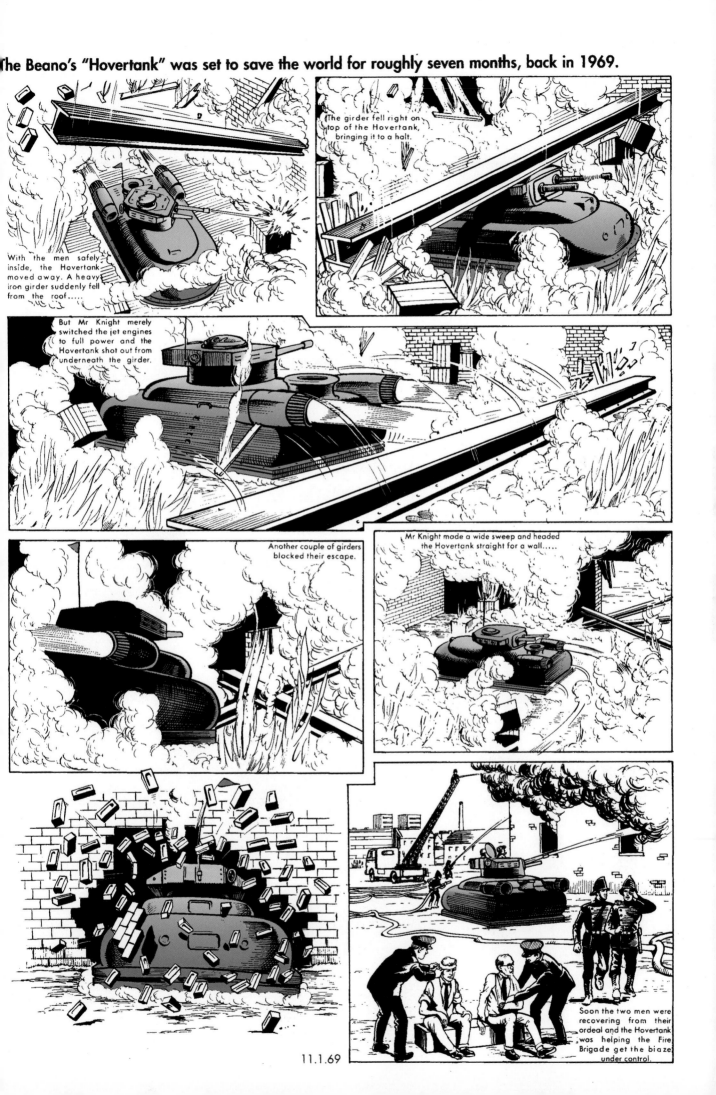

With the men safely inside, the Hovertank moved away. A heavy iron girder suddenly fell from the roof.....

The girder fell right on top of the Hovertank, bringing it to a halt.

But Mr Knight merely switched the jet engines to full power and the Hovertank shot out from underneath the girder.

Another couple of girders blocked their escape.

Mr Knight made a wide sweep and headed the Hovertank straight for a wall.....

Soon the two men were recovering from their ordeal and the Hovertank was helping the Fire Brigade get the blaze under control.

11.1.69

THE 3 BEARS once had, as guests on their page, **COLONEL CRACKPOT'S CIRCUS**, whose story, on another occasion, was invaded by **THE BASH STREET KIDS**, who had at one time invited **DENNIS THE MENACE** to help them. He also appeared in a **PUP PARADE** adventure, and they even had a visit from **MINNIE THE MINX**.

She invited, amongst others, **BILLY WHIZZ** to

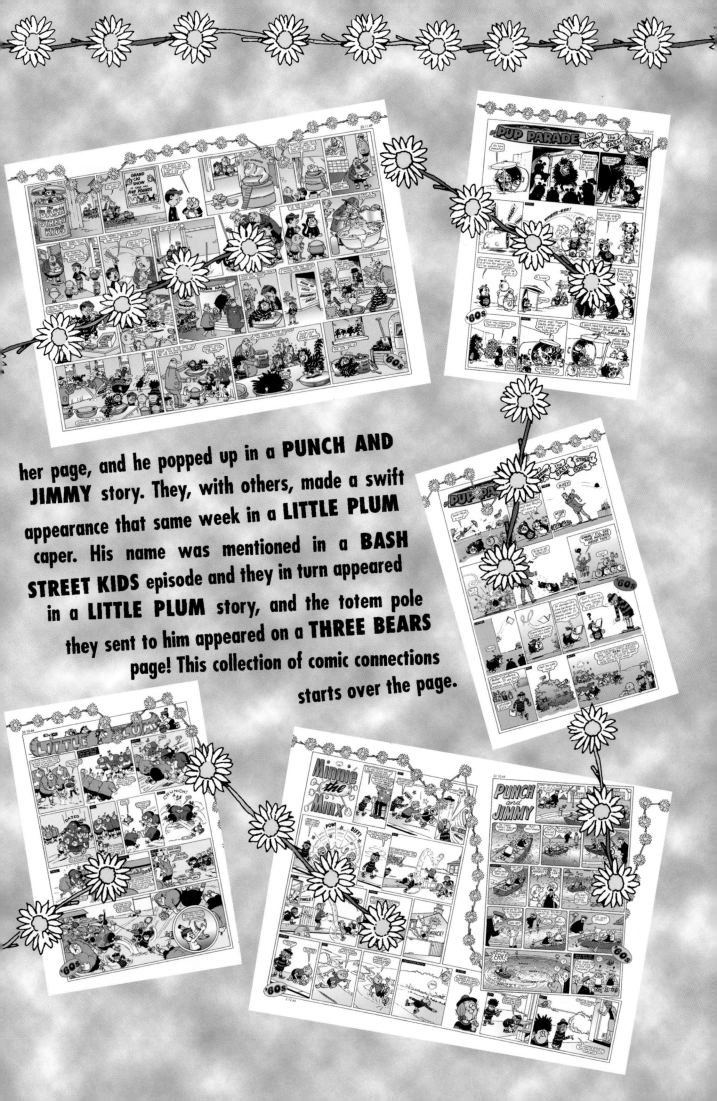

her page, and he popped up in a PUNCH AND JIMMY story. They, with others, made a swift appearance that same week in a LITTLE PLUM caper. His name was mentioned in a BASH STREET KIDS episode and they in turn appeared in a LITTLE PLUM story, and the totem pole they sent to him appeared on a THREE BEARS page! This collection of comic connections starts over the page.

23.8.69

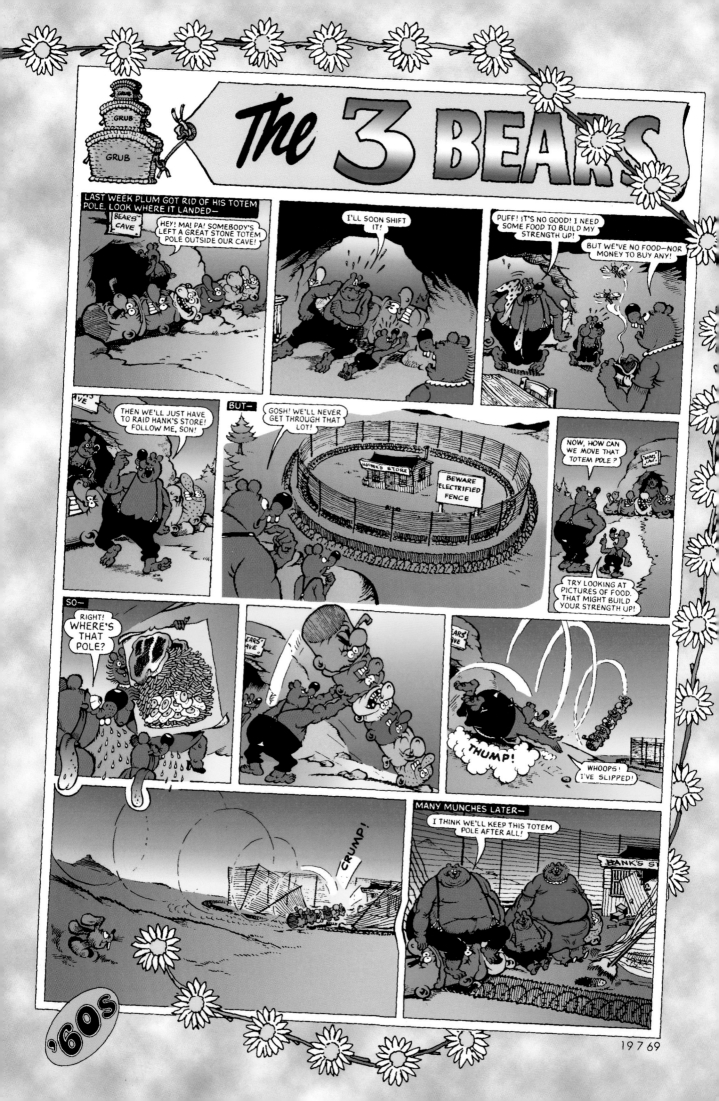

Biffo's cooked up a little problem for himself.
But, look — HAT'S the way to solve it!

20.10.62

This isn't exactly a fashion story of the '60s, but was chosen to let you see what Dennis looks like when he's wearing something other than a striped jumper!

You'd think that the Bash Street Kids would be the last to know anything about 'pop art' — originated by Andy Warhol back in the Sixties — but maybe Smiffy knows more than he is telling (see pic 14!).

Here are a couple of stories with a twist – no, not an unexpected ending, but one of the dance crazes of the Sixties!

2.6.62

The fashion in the Dandy of the 'Sixties was for squirty flowers and exploding cigars — but it could also predict fashionable things for the future! Look at the third-last picture of this Big Head and Thick Head story and you'll spot an absolutely 'wizard' name!

A BEANO ~~WEEK~~

WEAK WITH LAUGHTER!

BIFF!

WHOP!

There's no room in this book for a Beano Calendar — they didn't go on sale until the 1980s — but here's a week's-worth of Beano stories from the '60s. Stop day-dreaming, and start day-reading!

GUMDAY

26.8.67

MUGSDAY

ROGER the DODGER

8.7.67

ZOOSDAY

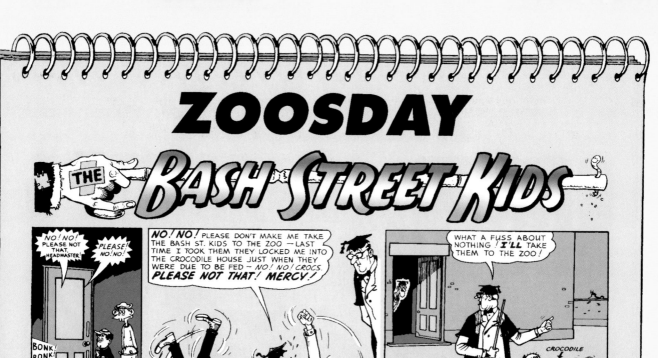

FISHINGSDAY

THIRSTDAY
The 3 BEARS
'60S

2.12.67

FIGHTDAY

PUNCH and JIMMY

30.9.67

SCATTERDAY

30.9.67

'60s

The next few pages illustrate some of the various vehicles to be found in the '60s (including a trip back in time to see a certain underwater craft), so we'll begin with a wily Winker Watson story, featuring a station wagon.

Winker WATSON

THE boys of the Third Form at Greytowers School were all very busy. They were washing their necks, polishing shoes, and generally sprucing themselves up — which was very unusual indeed. But then, today was the day when, along with the Third Form girls from Oak Lodge School next door, they had been invited to tea by the squire. However, at the last moment, Winker Watson, the champion wangler, heard that the girls wouldn't be going.

22.6.68

The HOVERCAR SNATCHERS

YOUNG Jinky Baker pelted across the tarmac at Shottenham Airport. Joe Casey, the famous football international, had been signed by an Italian club, and he was leaving for Rome on the noon plane. But Jinky meant to get his autograph before he went!

Jinky whirled round when a weird whining sound filled the air. Next second, a strange car with no wheels whizzed through the airport gates. Jinky gasped. It was the Hovercar! A few days before, two masked men had used it to kidnap a famous footballer. Were they after Jim Casey, too?

They were! The Hovercar slid to a halt near the plane. Blasts of compressed air sent Jinky and the other spectators flying. Out of the Hovercar sprang a burly masked man who grabbed Jim Casey, and bundled him into the Hovercar.

The doors of the Hovercar whirred shut—and the mystery car shot away. Straight across the runway it screamed — right into the path of a plane that was coming in to land!

"They're going to crash!" yelled Jinky. But no! At the last moment, the whine from the Hovercar grew louder. Powerful air jets blasted downwards, and the Hovercar rose and leapt over the plane like a gazelle. Then the amazing car sped on.

Jinky dashed across to a helicopter nearby. "Quick!" he told the pilot. "Joe Casey's been kidnapped. After that Hovercar!" "Right!" snapped Jim Braddock, the pilot. "Jump in!"

Within a minute they were airborne and climbing into the sky. "There it is!" yelled Jinky. The Hovercar was speeding away from the airport. At once Jim Braddock set off in pursuit.

an evil tale of masked men, a kidnapped footballer, and a beautifully-drawn steam train!

The Hovercar put on all speed, but it couldn't throw off its pursuers. Then suddenly the mystery men changed their tactics. The Hovercar left the road, went whizzing down an embankment — then swerved into a railway tunnel! "I'll fly over the hill and meet it at the other side," snapped Jim Braddock.

As the helicopter soared over the hill, Jinky yelled in dismay. "Look! There's a train coming!" he gasped. Sure enough, an express train was thundering down the line.

"It'll meet the Hovercar in the tunnel," gasped Jinky. "Joe Casey will be killed. We've got to stop that train!" Down swooped the helicopter. The crew of the engine gasped as it flew in close. Jinky and Jim yelled like mad—but it was useless. The train noises and the helicopter's engine drowned their voices. Into the tunnel plunged the train.

In the Hovercar, the kidnappers paled when they saw the approaching train. There was no room to pass. "We're gonna crash, boss!" gasped the bigger man.

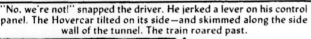

"No, we're not!" snapped the driver. He jerked a lever on his control panel. The Hovercar tilted on its side—and skimmed along the side wall of the tunnel. The train roared past.

Jinky and Jim Braddock gasped in amazement as the Hovercar shot from the tunnel. They could not understand how it had avoided a collision.

6.1.62

THE WOODEN SUBMARINE

MIKE and Ella Trubb were listening along with their Dad to the strangest escape plan ever proposed. Mr Trubb was an oil engineer in Borneo, which was being invaded by Japanese armies.

A Borneo barrelmaker called Seesaw had drawn up plans to build a wooden submarine, and in this remarkable craft, he told the Trubbs, they might escape to Australia!

Dad agreed—but very unwillingly. He doubted if the flimsy wooden craft could survive such a perilous voyage. Still, Seesaw set to work, aided by Mike and Ella, and the unusual craft soon began to take shape.

Already the Japanese were within striking distance. One of their planes zoomed over the harbour, gunning the Wooden Submarine.

Fortunately, Seesaw was able to repair the damage done by the bullets, but next day more raiders came. In a desperate attempt to prevent the submarine being holed again, Seesaw launched his craft—but that was a mistake!

Leaking badly, the submarine listed to one side then sank. Seesaw leaped clear! It seemed his clever invention was doomed.

People were leaving the island in all manner of boats. Now that the wooden sub was out of action, Mr Trubb hustled his children aboard the last junk. He would stay behind, but the youngsters must take their chance to escape.

Dandy 1969 — but WOOD it really work?

Loaded to the gunwales with its cargo of fugitives, the junk steered out to sea. There it was sighted by a Japanese bomber pilot.

Within minutes the bombs were raining down. Shattering explosions holed the junk.

Panic-stricken, the passengers leaped overboard. "Stay close!" Mike cried to Ella. They dived together. Both were strong swimmers.

When the junk broke up, Mike grabbed a piece of floating wreckage. They clung to it, and kicked out towards land.

Mike and Ella fought their way through the surf to make for the beach. Mike dragged his sister over the last few yards.

Bedraggled and soaked, they ran to the oil refinery, where their Dad was busy destroying the machinery. He turned in amazement when he heard their cry.

The engineer carried on with the job in hand—making the refinery useless for the enemy. As the flames roared, Dad ran with his youngsters.

Then, when it seemed that the Trubbs would have to remain on the island, they found fresh hope.

The amazing Seesaw had salvaged and repaired his tiny wooden submarine! Now the four daring adventurers loaded it up with stores.

They had to work fast. Japanese ships would be landing soldiers at any moment. While Dad worked the paddles, Mike kept watch through the conning-tower porthole.

All too soon, Mike reported an enemy gun-boat approaching the harbour. The wooden submarine submerged. Not a word was spoken. All aboard held their breath.

Slowly, steadily, noiselessly, the weird wooden submarine surged through the depths with its air-tube only inches above the surface. Unseen, it glided around the Japanese warship as the Japs opened fire on the abandoned port.

The fire blazed again. Out at sea the Wooden Submarine rose to the surface. Mike opened the hatch, and he and Ella looked back at what had been their homeland for so long. Their great journey to freedom had begun!

8.11.69

BRASSNECK

YESTERDAY morning, when Teacher Fatso Snodgrass came outside to ring the school bell, Charley Brand's amazing metal pal, Brassneck, grabbed it from him. The tin-can lad wanted to be helpful.

'60S

LET ME RING THE BELL FOR YOU, MR SNODGRASS!

HERE! HERE! NONE OF THAT!

DING! DING! DING!

But Brassneck's helpfulness went wrong. He gave the bell such a violent swing that it flew off the handle — and over the wall! Fatso flew off the handle, too!

YOU METAL MENACE! LOOK WHAT YOU'VE DONE!

Brassneck rushed to fetch the bell. But — calamity! It had been flattened by a six-ton road roller!

IS THAT YOUR BELL, MATE? I'M AFRAID I'VE JUST RUN OVER IT!

Fatso bellowed with rage.

YOU TIN-CAN VANDAL!

BUT IT STILL WORKS, MR SNODGRASS!

DONK! DONK!

Brassneck had to get out of punching range — and find a new bell.

YOU'LL BE SENT A BILL FOR THIS DAMAGE!

In the next street, the metal scallywag helped himself to the bell from a ragman's cart.

ANY OLD RAGS! GOOD PRICES PAID FOR OLD GOLD AND SILVER!

THIS IS THE VERY THING!

Proud as Punch, Brassneck strode into Fatso's class ringing his new bell.

HOW DO YOU LIKE THE TONE OF THIS BELL, MR SNODGRASS?

TING! TING! TING!

Unfortunately, the new bell did not bring pupils running. Instead, it brought the ragman's horse. Attracted by its master's bell, the animal peered in at the classroom window.

WHERE DID THAT NAG COME FROM?

IT ANSWERED THE BELL, SIR!

The horse wasn't on the school register, so it had to be expelled. And that wasn't easy!

I KNOW I'VE GOT A PACK OF ANIMALS IN MY CLASS, BUT I DRAW THE LINE AT A HORSE!

In the end, Brassneck had to go outside and drag the horse off by tugging at the cart.

GET THAT HORSE OUT OF HERE BEFORE I CALL FOR THE POLICE!

GOSH! MR SNODGRASS IS A VERY DIFFICULT MAN TO PLEASE!

A bell was still required. Brassneck "borrowed" one from the fire station!

FIRE STATION

THE FIRE BELL? I DON'T KNOW WHERE IT WENT. I HAVEN'T GOT IT!

The metal lad returned swiftly and cheerfully to let Fatso hear it ring.

I'VE BROUGHT YOU ANOTHER BELL, MR SNODGRASS!

WELL, I HOPE IT DOESN'T BRING SO MUCH TROUBLE AS THE LAST ONE!

DING-A-LING!

15.12.62

The speed record for motor scooters is thought to be held by an English woman who in 1965 ran her 200 cc Lambretta at over 130 mph on a racetrack at Monza, Italy. Perhaps Biffo won't scoot along so swiftly!

THE amazing story of William Grange, a schoolboy who has a secret identity — that of Billy the Cat, the mysterious crime-fighter of Burnham. One evening Billy is patrolling the roof-tops of the town when a voice hails him from the street below...

In the Beano of 1969, the towns of Burnham and Blackcastle must be within easy reach of each other, because the Hovertank's owner, Mr Knight, who lives in Blackcastle, has an urgent meeting with Billy the Cat in his home town of Burnham —

29.3.69

BILLY! BILLY THE CAT!

Billy quickly slithered down to find a worried Tom Knight, designer of the famous Hover-tank, waiting for him . . .

SOME CROOKS HAVE KIDNAPPED MY BOYS, KEVIN AND KENNETH, AND STOLEN THE HOVERTANK!

Mr Knight had been warned by the kid-nappers not to tell the police, or the boys would suffer.

I'VE GOT TO TAKE THE RANSOM TO BLACK ROCK TONIGHT.

HMM!

Billy thought deeply for a few minutes, then spoke quickly to Mr Knight.

Later that evening, Mr Knight's car approached Black Rock, out on the moors . . .

As Mr Knight placed the money in a hollow in the rock, Billy slid silently out of the boot.

Billy was well hidden by the time the car started back to Burnham.

Suddenly, the Hovertank roared out of a narrow gorge nearby.

HERE IT IS!

Billy knew the men. They were Stan Lawson and Bert Gibb, part of a gang of crooks run by Alan Robb.

As the Hovertank left, Billy jumped up from cover.

'60s

He dropped, silently, on to the turret.

Soon, the Hovertank reached its destination—a hut far out on Burnham Moor.

The two messengers were greeted by the other members of the gang, Sandy Baird and Alan Robb himself.

GOT THE CASH, EH?

Suddenly —

B-BILLY THE CAT!

Baird swung his fist, but . . .

. . . he was no match for a judo expert like Billy the Cat!

COME ON, KID—WE'RE GETTING OUT OF HERE!

Robb bundled Kevin into the Hovertank and started the motors and, at the roar of the jets, Billy rushed outside . . .

. . . but he was too late.

As the Hovertank raced out of the gully, Billy ran for the steep hillside.

By taking a short cut over the hill, Billy had got ahead of the stolen Hovertank.

GOOD! HERE IT COMES!

But, just as Billy was about to jump on the Hovertank, Robb spotted him.

Robb put the Hovertank into a swerve so that Billy missed.

Then the machine swung completely round and charged at Billy . . .

But Robb had forgotten about Billy's wonderful agility.

The crook panicked . . .

He jumped from the fast-moving vehicle.

But the Hovertank had stampeded a herd of cattle . . .

GET TO THE CONTROLS, KEVIN!

H-HELP!

. . . and Robb was directly in their path!

SWING THE TURRET ROUND!

Billy had grabbed the crook in the nick of time.

Meanwhile, Tom Knight, designer of the famous Hovertank and father of the twins, had told the Burnham police about the kidnapping and Billy's rescue attempt.

WE'LL HAVE TO SEARCH THE WHOLE MOOR!

Suddenly —

LOOK!

Billy and Kevin had returned to the crooks' hut on the moor, freed Kenneth and brought the kidnappers back.

Shortly after, Billy was home changing to his other identity, that of William Grange, a seemingly quiet schoolboy.

Next day, at Burnham Academy —

THE HOVERTANK WAS IN TOWN TODAY WITH BILLY THE CAT, WILLIAM — PITY YOU MISSED THEM!

ER-YES!

'60S

Minnie the Minx and dressmaking don't mix in this 1967 tale — until she gets an idea from another Beano character that "suits" her!

Down below, the Bash Street Pups have a similar idea . . . meet 'Sniffy the Cat'!

SEE THE HOVERTANK ELSEWHERE IN THE BOOK.

25.11.67

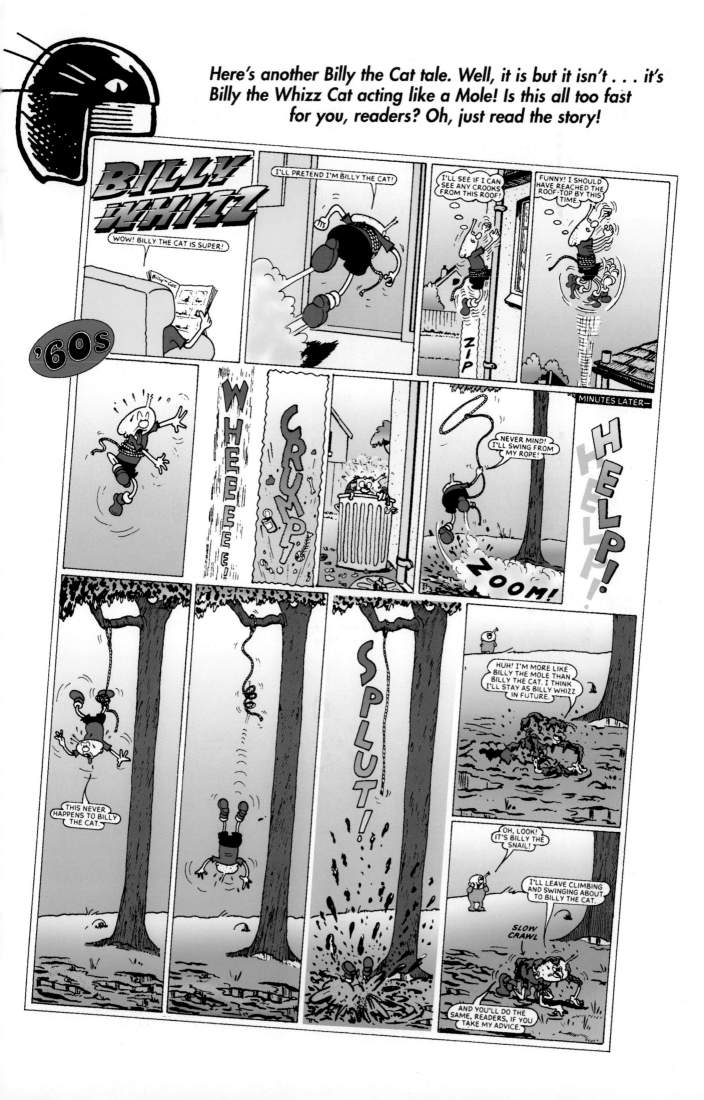

NUTSDAY

9.1.65

NOMONEYDAY

22.6.68

TATTOOSDAY

RIBBONSDAY

THIRSTDAY

THE

Dandy

3°

EVERY TUESDAY. No. 1206—JAN, 2nd. 1965.

'60s

2.1.65

FLYDAY

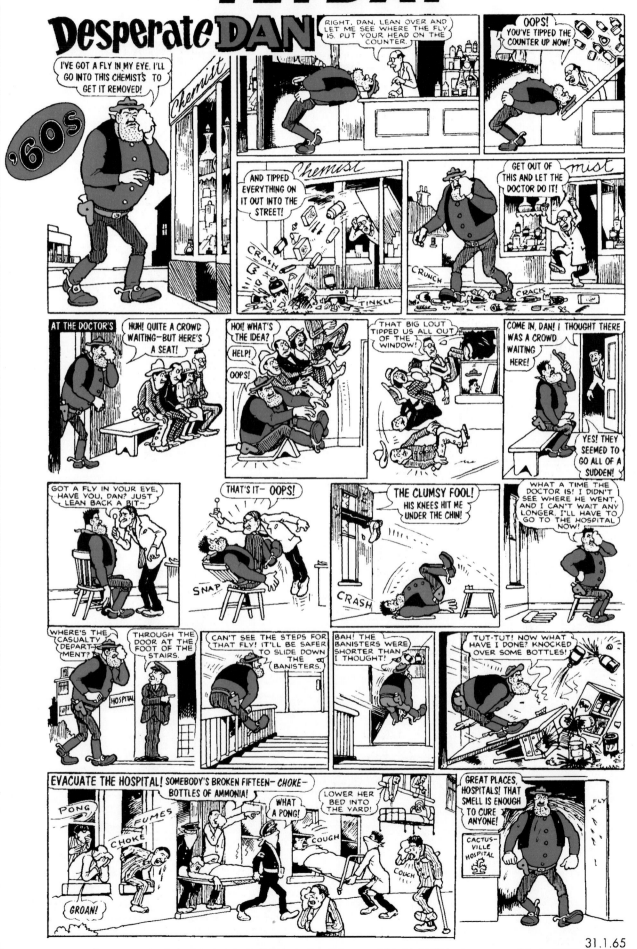

SPLATDIRTDAY

Just a couple of years ago someone came up with the idea of a washing machine for dogs, where the dog is sprayed with water in a large metal container, complete with window, so the dog can keep an eye on his owner! Well, the idea isn't so new after all, as this Biffo The Bear from 1969 demonstrates — although Professor Screwtopp's machine doesn't have a window!

RED RORY OF THE EAGLES

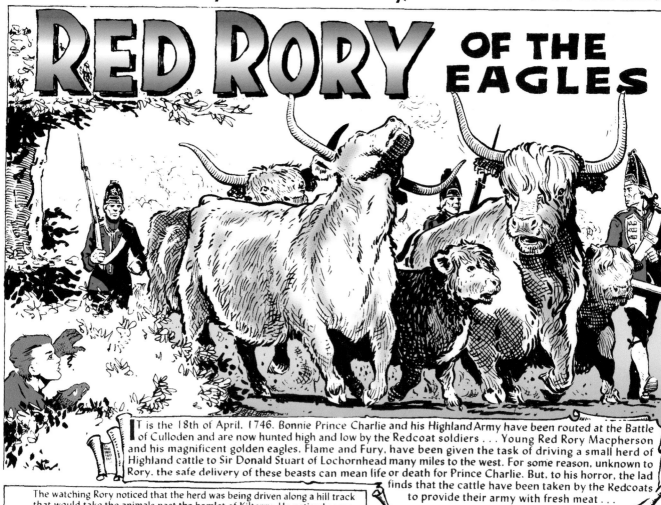

IT is the 18th of April, 1746. Bonnie Prince Charlie and his Highland Army have been routed at the Battle of Culloden and are now hunted high and low by the Redcoat soldiers . . . Young Red Rory Macpherson and his magnificent golden eagles, Flame and Fury, have been given the task of driving a small herd of Highland cattle to Sir Donald Stuart of Lochornhead many miles to the west. For some reason, unknown to Rory, the safe delivery of these beasts can mean life or death for Prince Charlie. But, to his horror, the lad finds that the cattle have been taken by the Redcoats to provide their army with fresh meat . . .

The watching Rory noticed that the herd was being driven along a hill track that would take the animals past the hamlet of Kilterry. He noticed something else — those cattle seemed thirsty, and that sparked off a plan in Rory's mind. But he would have to get to Kilterry before the herd. Calling the eagles, he raced like a deer across country.

Rory arrived at Kilterry while the cattle were still half a mile away. Now he would need the villagers' help . .

Ten minutes later the herd and its Redcoat drovers plodded down the narrow village street. Of Rory and the eagles there was no sign.

Then the thirsty beasts scented water and headed at a trot towards the village well.

Suddenly, with harsh cries, Flame and Fury flew up from the well brushing the muzzles of the cattle with their great wings. Then Rory, too, appeared out of the well.

Bellowing with terror the startled beasts wheeled and stampeded down the narrow street, bowling over the Redcoats like ninepins. Rory, chuckling at the success of his plan, raced after the thundering herd.

In obedience to Rory's shrill cries the eagles shepherded the beasts down a side track that led into the hills. Suddenly the boy heard the crack of a musket shot and a split second later felt a searing pain in his leg.

As Flame and Fury turned to attack the soldier who had fired at their young master. Rory's heart sank. Now he could not hope to drive the herd away into the hills—the pain in his wounded leg was so great that he could barely hobble. Then he heard a soft whisper from a nearby cottage window. It was his friend, Donald Fraser, one of the villagers.

ALL IS NOT LOST, LAD. COME INTO MY COTTAGE.

In a few minutes the Redcoats had recovered and, led by their corporal, they pounded in pursuit of the herd.

They charged into the side-track— and stopped, gaping. The hill road leading from the village was empty as far as the eye could see . . .

And no wonder! The wounded Rory, Donald and the eagles, had driven the cattle into Donald's cottage. But the danger was not yet over. Donald, his body blocking the window, was spotted by the Redcoat corporal who moved over to question the High-lander. Rory held his breath. One stamp of a hoof, or one cry from a frightened child, would mean disaster.

WHERE ARE THE CATTLE, HIGHLANDER? SPEAK THE TRUTH IF YOU VALUE YOUR LIFE . . . .

26.5.62

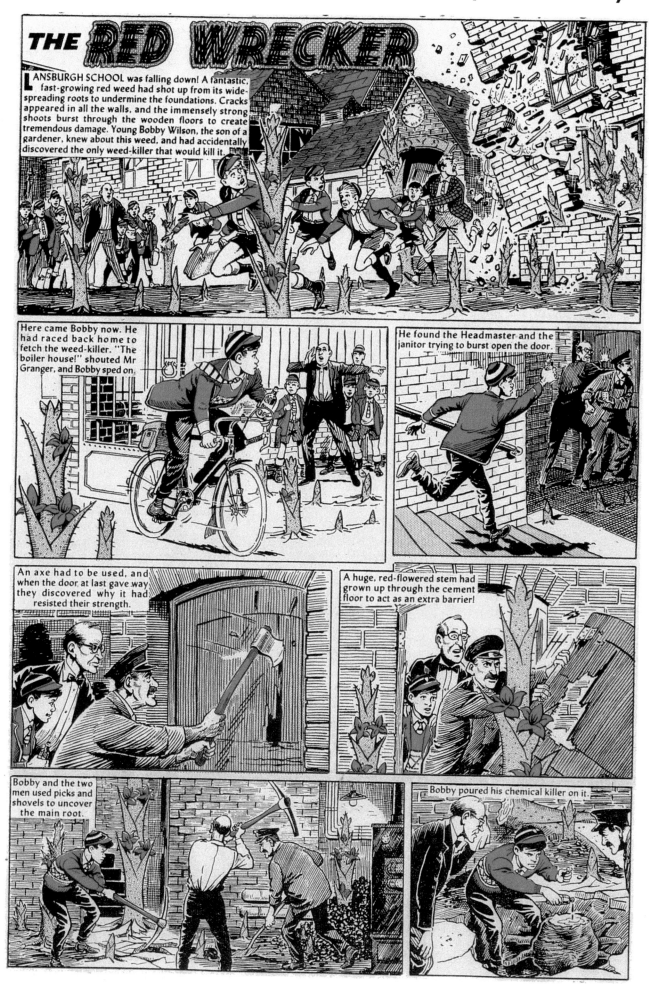

cautionary tale to all growers of hybrid plants . . .

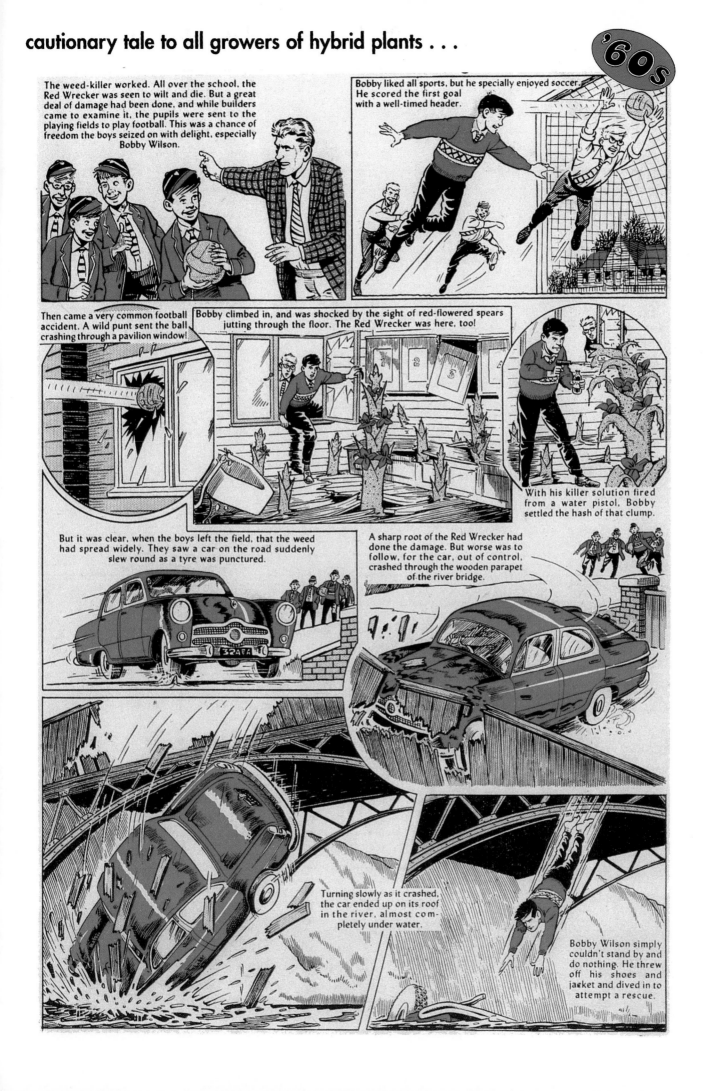

The weed-killer worked. All over the school, the Red Wrecker was seen to wilt and die. But a great deal of damage had been done, and while builders came to examine it, the pupils were sent to the playing fields to play football. This was a chance of freedom the boys seized on with delight, especially Bobby Wilson.

Bobby liked all sports, but he specially enjoyed soccer. He scored the first goal with a well-timed header.

Then came a very common football accident. A wild punt sent the ball crashing through a pavilion window!

Bobby climbed in, and was shocked by the sight of red-flowered spears jutting through the floor. The Red Wrecker was here, too!

With his killer solution fired from a water pistol, Bobby settled the hash of that clump.

But it was clear, when the boys left the field, that the weed had spread widely. They saw a car on the road suddenly slew round as a tyre was punctured.

A sharp root of the Red Wrecker had done the damage. But worse was to follow, for the car, out of control, crashed through the wooden parapet of the river bridge.

Turning slowly as it crashed, the car ended up on its roof in the river, almost completely under water.

Bobby Wilson simply couldn't stand by and do nothing. He threw off his shoes and jacket and dived in to attempt a rescue.

It took almost all the boy's strength to haul the drowning man from inside.

His school pals were ready to help, and they tried to revive the unconscious driver.

While Bobby dried his clothes by a fire where two men were digging for a root of the Red Wrecker, he suddenly thought of something that had to be done at once.

ROAD WORK

Racing home, he entered the garden shed. He was going to burn up that packet of foreign seed that had given birth to the Red Wrecker.

The seeds were gone! Bobby was completely puzzled. Who had taken them? And why?

Down at the river that night, a man who had very nearly been drowned returned to the scene of his accident. He groped inside the crashed car.

When he waded towards the bank again, the mystery man was pocketing a square package taken from the car.

And down at a jeweller's store in Lansburgh a shadowy figure watched more red shoots thrusting up through the pavement! It was he who had sown some seeds here!

JEW

In the middle of the night a week later Bobby Wilson was awakened by Constable Carstairs, who knew that the red weed had first appeared in the Wilson garden. "Look!" he said at the river bank. Bobby stared in horror. The sunken car could be seen again, borne upwards on the thrusting stems of the Red Wrecker!

20.9.64

The vehicle in this 'odd-ball' story was described as "a tank without caterpillar tracks" and "an armoured car without wheels" but Dandy readers in 1963/64 knew it as . . .

The Crimson Ball

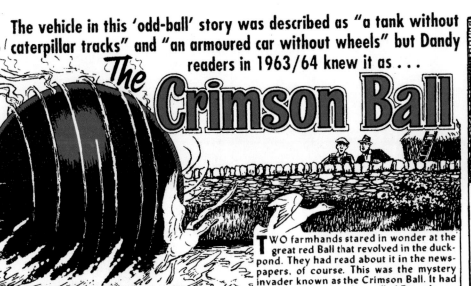

TWO farmhands stared in wonder at the great red Ball that revolved in the duckpond. They had read about it in the newspapers, of course. This was the mystery invader known as the Crimson Ball. It had been set on fire by a boy called Peter Jones, and now it was cooling down.

Now the Master of the Crimson Ball seemed to be in a fury. The Ball came hurtling after the boy, who had reached the rear door of a cinema. In sheer desperation, he burst the door open.

But he had barely got inside and turned from the side passage to the middle one when the Crimson Ball came after him—bursting through a brick wall and through the cinema screen to get at him!

The audience panicked, screaming in fear as each and every one scrambled to get out of the way. Seats were buckled and crushed as the Crimson Ball pursued Peter.

Peter reached the open air only a few yards ahead. Turning, he threw his last bottle of chemical mixture. If this one didn't work, his number was up.

But, wonder of wonders! The Crimson Ball burst into flames as the bottle shattered against it! Peter's heart leapt. He had found the stuff that would destroy the Ball!

Almost at once hope turned to despair, for several well-meaning citizens sprang to action. There was danger that the burning Ball would set the whole street ablaze, so two men turned fire extinguishers on it, while another phoned for help.

"No! Let it burn!" yelled Peter frantically.

The men wouldn't listen to him. In a few minutes the fire brigade was at work, reeling out hoses and playing jets on the burning Crimson Ball. In sheer desperation, Peter ran towards a fire engine to stop the firemen's work.

Snatching a fireman's axe, Peter sprang to the nearest line of hose and cleaved it clean through. An angry fireman leaped to grab him.

'60s

There was still a chance, Peter thought. He wriggled free.

He pelted off towards the smoking hot Crimson Ball.

This time Peter was after the broken bottle. On its label were details of the chemicals which had set the Ball on fire, and Peter must get it to restart the blaze.

Now the Ball came rolling after its chief enemy, the boy who knew the secret of how to set it on fire.

When Peter slipped through a fence and crossed the main road, the Crimson Ball caused havoc amongst the traffic. A lorry was knocked spinning and a car crashed into it. Another car slewed into a ditch to avoid the Ball. Peter ran on, clutching his bottle.

When a canvas-roofed lorry passed him, the boy took a desperate chance. He tossed the broken bottle on to its roof.

Before the Crimson Ball could overtake the lorry, a canal bridge opened to let a barge through. Foiled, the Ball went after Peter again. But he had in the meantime taken his chance to write a note to the police.

In the main street of the little town, as the Crimson Ball approached, Peter hurled a stone through a jeweller's window. His note was tied to it—and this was Peter's way of making sure the police got his message.

But now he was at the mercy of the Crimson Ball. It was right on his heels— and presently it gave him his orders.

"Lead the way to Farnbury Aerodrome," commanded the Master. "Try any tricks and you'll be crushed to death!"

4.1.64

23.8.69